Comfort

Comfort

THE SMALL PRINT

EGGS We use medium eggs, unless otherwise stated. Pregnant women, the elderly and children should avoid recipes with eggs which are raw or not fully cooked if not produced under the British Lion code of practice.

FRUIT AND VEGETABLES Recipes use medium-size fruit and veg, unless otherwise stated.

REDUCED-FAT SOFT CHEESE Where a recipe uses reduced-fat soft cheese, we mean a soft cheese with 30% less fat than its full-fat equivalent.

LOW-FAT SPREAD When a recipe uses a low-fat spread, we mean a spread with a fat content of no more than 39%.

MICROWAVES If we have used a microwave in any of our recipes, the timings will be for an 850-watt microwave oven.

PREP AND COOK TIMES These are approximate and meant to be guidelines only. Prep time includes all steps up to and following the main cooking time(s). Stated cook times may vary according to your oven.

VEGETARIAN ITALIAN-STYLE HARD CHEESE Where we reference this in vegetarian recipes, we mean a cheese similar to parmesan (which is not vegetarian) but which is suitable for vegetarians.

GLUTEN FREE Recipes labelled as gluten free include ingredients that naturally do not contain gluten, but may also contain processed products, such as sauces, stock cubes and spice mixes. If so, you should ensure that those products do not include any gluten-containing ingredients (wheat, barley or rye) – these will be highlighted in the ingredients list on the product label. Manufacturers may also indicate whether there is a chance their product may have been accidentally contaminated with gluten during the manufacturing process. For more information and guidance on gluten-free products, visit www.coeliac.org.uk

SmartPoints® have been calculated using the values for generic foods, not brands (except where stated). Tracking using branded items may affect the recorded SmartPoints.

Seven c3

Produced by Seven Publishing on behalf of Weight Watchers International, Inc. Published October 2018. All rights reserved. No part of this publication may be reproduced, stored in a retrieval system or transmitted in any form by any means, electronic, mechanical photocopying, recording or otherwise, without the prior written permission of Seven Publishing. First published in Great Britain by Seven Publishing Ltd.

Seven Publishing Ltd, 3-7 Herbal Hill, London EC1R 5EJ
www.seven.co.uk

This book is copyright under the Berne Convention. No reproduction without permission. All rights reserved.

10 9 8 7 6 5 4 3 2 1

© 2018 WW International, Inc. All rights reserved. The SmartPoints Weight-Loss System and these materials are proprietary to WW International, Inc. and are licensed to WW members solely for their personal use in losing and controlling their weight. Any other use, including but not limited to reproduction or distribution in any form or medium, is strictly prohibited. NOT FOR RESALE. WEIGHT WATCHERS, the WW Logo, POINTS and SmartPoints are the registered trademarks of WW International, Inc.

A CIP catalogue record for this book is available from the British Library.

ISBN: 978-1-9996673-1-3

WEIGHT WATCHERS PUBLICATIONS TEAM
Samantha Rees, Nicola Hill, Ruby Bamford, Kim Clayden

FOR SEVEN PUBLISHING LTD
FOOD
Food editor: Nadine Brown
Associate food editor: Ella Tarn

EDITORIAL
Editor-in-Chief: Helen Renshaw
Editor: Ward Hellewell
Sub-editors: Sarah Nittinger, Julie Stevens

DESIGN & PHOTOGRAPHY
Art director: Liz Baird
Photography: Kris Kirkham
Food stylists: Catherine Hill, Amber De Florio
Prop stylist: Tamzin Ferdinando

ACCOUNT MANAGEMENT
Account manager: Gina Cavaciuti
Group publishing director: Kirsten Price

PRODUCTION
Production director: Liz Knipe
Colour reproduction by F1 Colour
Printed in the UK by CPI Colour

Contents

Nostalgic toad in the hole, warming chicken and vegetable soup or heavenly fruit trifle – our WW Kitchen Team love good food and the way it can make you feel. In this collection of more than 60 delicious recipes, we've taken some of your best-loved dishes and given them a WW makeover, meaning you can cook and enjoy them with your family and friends – and stay on track. So if you thought mac 'n' cheese, fish and chips or steamed pudding and custard were off limits, you may be surprised when you take a look inside. From fast food and family favourites to meat-free meals and sweet treats, all the recipes have been tried and tested to ensure they're simple to make and delicious to eat. So gather round the table and serve up feel-good food that's guaranteed to put a smile on everyone's faces.

WHEN YOU SEE THESE SYMBOLS:

4   Tells you the SmartPoints value per serving.

     Indicates a recipe is gluten free (see page 6).

     Indicates a recipe is vegetarian.

     Indicates a recipe is vegan.

Family favourites

Toad in the hole

serves 4   prep time 10 minutes   cook time 45 minutes

A favourite with kids and adults alike, this classic dish is sure to take you back to your childhood. Try serving it with steamed cabbage and tasty mustard gravy.

8 reduced-fat pork sausages
125g plain flour
2 eggs
200ml skimmed milk
2 tablespoons sunflower oil
300g shallots, halved, if large
6 fresh sage leaves
320g Savoy cabbage, leaves separated, trimmed and roughly chopped

FOR THE GRAVY
2 tablespoons gravy granules
1 teaspoon wholegrain mustard

1 Heat the grill to medium-high and cook the sausages for 15 minutes, turning occasionally until cooked through.

2 In a mixing bowl, whisk together the flour, eggs and milk, then season to taste and set aside in the fridge until needed.

3 Preheat the oven to 200°C, fan 180°C, gas mark 6. Put ½ tablespoon of the oil into a large, nonstick frying pan and set over a medium heat. Add the shallots and cook for 10 minutes until softened and golden.

4 Put the remaining oil into a 2-litre baking dish and put in the oven for 3-4 minutes until the oil is very hot. Remove from the oven and pour in the batter, then top with the sausages, shallots and sage, return to the oven and bake for 25-30 minutes until golden and risen.

5 Meanwhile, cook the cabbage in a pan of boiling water for 3-5 minutes, or until just tender, then drain well.

6 To make the gravy, whisk the granules into 200ml boiling water in a small jug until smooth and thickened, adding a little extra water if needed. Stir in the mustard. Serve the toad in the hole with the cabbage and gravy on the side.

Cook's tip
You could serve this with 125g boiled new potatoes per person, for an extra 3 SmartPoints per serving.

10 SmartPoints value per serving

Simple fish pie

serves 6   freezable   prep time 15 minutes   cook time 50 minutes

There are lots of variations on this popular dish – this version uses sliced potatoes, rather than mash, which go all golden and crispy when the pie is baked.

2 x 250g potatoes
Calorie controlled cooking spray
1 onion, thinly sliced
3 tablespoons plain flour
300ml semi-skimmed milk
2 x 300g packs fish pie mix
200g frozen garden peas
15g low-fat spread, melted
200g Tenderstem broccoli

1   Preheat the oven to 200°C, fan 180°C, gas mark 6. Bring a large pan of water to the boil and add the whole potatoes. Cook for 3-4 minutes until you can just prick them with a fork – they don't need to be cooked through. Drain and allow to cool, then slice into 3-4mm rounds and set aside.

2   Mist a pan with cooking spray and put over a medium heat. Add the onion and cook for 6-8 minutes, or until soft.

3   Add the flour, stir well and cook for 1 minute. Reduce the heat and gradually add the milk. Simmer, stirring constantly, for 5 minutes until the sauce has thickened.

4   Remove the pan from the heat and stir in the fish pie mix and the peas. Season to taste, then pour into a 2-litre oval pie dish. Top with the sliced potatoes, brush with the melted spread and season with freshly ground black pepper.

5   Put the dish on a baking sheet and bake for 35-40 minutes until the potatoes are golden and the fish is cooked through.

6   Meanwhile, cook the broccoli in a pan of boiling water for 3-4 minutes until tender. Drain and serve with the fish pie.

The fish pie can be frozen in an airtight container for up to 3 months.

4 SmartPoints value per serving

Tuna pasta bake

serves 6   prep time 15 minutes   cook time 35 minutes

This delicious pasta bake is a guaranteed winner with all the family. You can have it on the table in less than an hour, so it makes a great midweek meal.

350g rigatoni pasta

1 slice Weight Watchers Malted Danish Bread

25g low-fat spread

25g plain flour

400ml skimmed milk

130g half-fat Cheddar cheese, grated

2 x 160g tins tuna in spring water, drained and flaked

340g tin sweetcorn, drained

3 spring onions, trimmed and thinly sliced

Calorie controlled cooking spray

Salad leaves, to serve

1 Preheat the oven to 200°C, fan 180°C, gas mark 6. Bring a large pan of salted water to the boil and add the pasta. Cook for 10-12 minutes until just al dente – you don't want it to be overcooked. Drain, reserving a little of the pasta water.

2 Meanwhile, blitz the bread in a food processor to make breadcrumbs.

3 Melt the spread in a large pan, stir in the flour and cook for 1 minute over a medium heat. Add a splash of the milk and stir to loosen the paste, then gradually stir in the rest of the milk using a wooden spoon. Cook for 5 minutes, stirring often, until the sauce is thick enough to coat the back of the spoon. Remove from the heat and stir in half the cheese. Season to taste.

4 Add the pasta, tuna, sweetcorn and spring onions to the sauce. If it seems too thick, add a splash of the reserved pasta water to loosen it. Pour the mixture into a 2-litre ovenproof dish. Combine the remaining cheese with the breadcrumbs and scatter over the top. Mist the top with cooking spray, then bake for 15-20 minutes until golden. Serve with the salad leaves.

 **9   SmartPoints value per serving**

Cottage pie

serves 6   freezable   prep time 15 minutes   cook time 1 hour

A great British classic, the humble cottage pie makes a brilliant all-in-one meal.
Or, you can serve it with extra veg like we have here – peas are perfect!

**750g Maris Piper potatoes,
quartered**

**1 small cauliflower, trimmed and
cut into florets**

Calorie controlled cooking spray

1 onion, finely diced

2 carrots, finely diced

2 celery sticks, finely diced

2 garlic cloves, finely chopped

**500g 5% fat extra lean
beef mince**

1 tablespoon tomato purée

400g tin chopped tomatoes

1 bay leaf

1 beef stock cube

400g frozen garden peas

50g low-fat spread

1 Cook the potatoes in a large pan of boiling water for 10 minutes. Add the cauliflower and cook for 8-10 minutes or until everything is soft. Drain and set aside in the covered pan.

2 Meanwhile, mist a large pan with cooking spray and put over a medium heat. Add the onion, carrots, celery and garlic, and cook for 6-8 minutes until soft. Add the beef and cook for 4-5 minutes, or until it is brown and cooked through.

3 Preheat the oven to 180°C, fan 160°C, gas mark 4. Add the tomato purée, tomatoes and bay leaf to the mince mixture and season well. Crumble in the stock cube, then stir in 300ml water and bring to the boil. Reduce the heat and simmer for 15 minutes until the sauce has reduced and thickened. Add 100g of the peas, stir through and cook for a further minute. Remove and discard the bay leaf.

4 Mash the potatoes and cauliflower with the low-fat spread and season to taste. Pour the mince mixture into 6 individual ovenproof pie dishes and top with the mash, using a fork to spread it evenly. Bake for 20-25 minutes or until golden.

5 About 5 minutes before the end of cooking time, cook the remaining peas in a pan of water for 3 minutes, then serve with the cottage pie.

The cottage pie can be frozen in an airtight container for up to 3 months.

Cook's tip

If you don't want to make individual pies, you can make one large one – just use a 2-litre ovenproof baking dish.

6 **SmartPoints value per serving**

Easy chicken & mushroom pie

serves 6   prep time 20 minutes   cook time 50 minutes

A hearty pie is a real treat on a chilly evening. This one has a tasty chicken and mushroom filling, topped with light puff pastry.

15g low-fat spread

2 leeks, trimmed and thickly sliced

250g chestnut mushrooms, thickly sliced

3 tablespoons plain flour

300ml chicken stock, made with 1 stock cube

150g half-fat crème fraîche

1 tablespoon wholegrain mustard

300g cooked skinless chicken breast, shredded

Small handful fresh tarragon, leaves picked and roughly chopped

225g ready-rolled light puff pastry

1 egg, lightly beaten

400g new potatoes

300g green beans, trimmed

1   Preheat the oven to 220°C, fan 200°C, gas mark 7.

2   Melt the spread in a pan over a medium heat. Add the leeks and mushrooms and cook for 5 minutes, or until softened. Season to taste, then stir in the flour and cook for 2 minutes. Gradually add the stock, followed by the crème fraîche. Cook for 5 minutes on a low heat, stirring often, until the sauce has thickened, then stir in the wholegrain mustard.

3   Stir the chicken and tarragon into the sauce, then spoon the mixture into a 23cm round pie dish. Top with the pastry, pressing it along the edge of the dish to seal and trimming off and discarding any excess. Cut a small cross in the centre of the pastry, then brush all over with the beaten egg.

4   Bake for 35 minutes, or until the pastry is golden.

5   Meanwhile, cook the new potatoes in a pan of boiling water for 10 minutes. Add the beans for the last 5 minutes of cooking time. Drain the vegetables and serve with the pie.

9   SmartPoints value per serving

Chicken & vegetable soup

serves 6   freezable   prep time 15 minutes   cook time 1 hour 20 minutes

Nothing warms the heart quite like a big bowl of chicken soup. This one has green lentils and lots of extra veg to make it even more satisfying.

Calorie controlled cooking spray
5 garlic cloves, finely sliced
2 onions, cut into thin wedges
4 carrots, sliced diagonally
4 celery sticks, thickly sliced
2 bay leaves
A few sprigs fresh thyme
2.5 litres chicken stock, made with 2 stock cubes
3 skinless chicken breast fillets
150g dried green lentils, rinsed
150g kale, thick stalks removed and discarded, and leaves chopped
Juice of ½ lemon

1   Mist a large, deep pan with cooking spray and put over a medium-high heat. Add the garlic, onion, carrots and celery and cook for 2-3 minutes, then add the bay leaves, thyme and stock. Bring to the boil, then reduce the heat, cover and simmer for 45 minutes.

2   Add the chicken fillets and lentils, making sure the chicken is covered by the broth. Cook for 15-20 minutes until the chicken is cooked through. Remove the chicken and set aside to cool slightly. Cook the soup for another 5 minutes, or until the lentils are tender.

3   Shred the chicken and return it to the soup, along with the kale. Stir to combine, then simmer for 5 minutes until the kale is wilted. Add the lemon juice, season to taste and serve.

The soup can be frozen in an airtight container for up to 3 months.

0 **SmartPoints value per serving**

Cook's tip
Serve this with a toasted sandwich thin each for an extra 3 SmartPoints per serving.

Roast pork with onion gravy

serves 4   prep time 20 minutes   cook time 1 hour 5 minutes

A traditional Sunday roast is hard to beat. This version uses pork tenderloin with herbs, honey and mustard adding loads of flavour.

4 carrots, cut into 1cm chunks

2 red onions, cut into wedges

600g new potatoes, halved or quartered, if large

2 apples, cored and cut into wedges

3 garlic cloves

1½ tablespoons wholegrain mustard

2 teaspoons clear honey

500ml chicken stock, made with 1 stock cube

1 tablespoon dried mixed herbs

Grated zest of 1 lemon

400g pork tenderloin fillet

Calorie controlled cooking spray

4 tablespoons onion chutney

2 teaspoons cornflour

1   Preheat the oven to 190°C, fan 170°C, gas mark 5. Put the vegetables, apples and garlic cloves in a roasting tin. In a small jug, combine the mustard with the honey and 150ml of the chicken stock, then pour over the vegetables. Season to taste, cover with foil and roast for 25 minutes.

2   Meanwhile, put a frying pan over a medium heat. Mix the dried herbs with the lemon zest and some salt and pepper on a dinner plate. Mist the pork with cooking spray, then roll it in the herb mixture. Put the pork in the pan and cook, turning, for 5 minutes until browned all over.

3   Take the roasting tin with the vegetables out of the oven and remove the foil. Put the pork on top of the veg and return the tin, uncovered, to the oven. Increase the temperature to 200°C, fan 180°C, gas mark 6 and roast for 40 minutes or until the pork is cooked to your liking.

4   Meanwhile, make the onion gravy. Put the onion chutney and remaining stock in a small pan and put over a low-medium heat. In a small jug, combine the cornflour with 4 teaspoons of water and add to the pan. Simmer, whisking constantly, for 2-3 minutes, or until thickened.

5   Slice the pork and serve with the vegetables and gravy.

8   **SmartPoints value per serving**

Beef stroganoff with celeriac mash

serves 4   freezable   prep time 20 minutes   cook time 30 minutes

Tender beef, chestnut mushrooms and paprika combine in this delicious Russian stew that's made even more luxurious with a dollop of crème fraîche.

**1 small celeriac, peeled and
cut into chunks**

40g low-fat spread

1 teaspoon vegetable oil

300g thin-cut lean sirloin steak

1 onion, thinly sliced

2 garlic cloves, finely chopped

1 tablespoon paprika

**1 green pepper, deseeded
and sliced**

400g chestnut mushrooms, sliced

**150ml beef stock, made
with 1 stock cube**

Juice of ½ lemon

1 teaspoon Dijon mustard

300g green beans, trimmed

125g half-fat crème fraîche

1   Put the celeriac in a pan of water and bring to the boil. Reduce the heat and simmer for 25-30 minutes until tender all the way through. Drain, then return the celeriac to the pan with the low-fat spread, season to taste and mash until smooth.

2   Meanwhile, heat the oil in a nonstick frying pan and add the steak. Cook for 1-2 minutes on each side until seared, but don't cook it through – it should still be rare inside. Transfer to a plate and set aside.

3   Add the onion to the pan and cook for 6-8 minutes, until softened but not coloured. Add the garlic and paprika, and cook for 1-2 minutes until fragrant. Add the pepper and chestnut mushrooms and fry for 5-6 minutes until softened.

4   Add the beef stock, lemon juice and mustard, and simmer for 1 minute. Slice the steak into strips and add to the pan with all its juices, then simmer for 3 minutes until just cooked through.

5   Meanwhile, cook the green beans in a pan of boiling water for 4-5 minutes until just tender, then drain.

6   Stir the crème fraîche into the stroganoff and season to taste. Serve with the celeriac mash and green beans.

The stroganoff can be frozen in an airtight container for up to 3 months.

6   **SmartPoints value per serving**

Turkey lasagne

serves 6   freezable   prep time 20 minutes   cook time 1 hour 20 minutes

Lasagne is always a crowd-pleaser and if you have leftovers it's easy to freeze and reheat. This flavour-packed recipe uses turkey mince instead of the usual beef.

Calorie controlled cooking spray
500g turkey breast mince
1 onion, finely diced
3 cloves garlic, finely chopped
1 teaspoon dried mixed herbs
2 teaspoons fennel seeds
2 bay leaves
400g tin chopped tomatoes
1 tablespoon tomato purée
25g low-fat spread
25g plain flour
350ml skimmed milk
200g ricotta
¼ teaspoon ground nutmeg
6 dried lasagna sheets
125g light mozzarella, sliced
20g grated Parmesan
Small handful fresh basil leaves, to garnish
80g Italian-style salad leaves, to serve

1   Mist a large pan with cooking spray and put over a medium-high heat. Add the turkey mince and onion and cook for 5 minutes until the mince is cooked through.

2   Add the garlic, mixed herbs, fennel seeds and bay leaves and cook for 1 minute. Stir in the chopped tomatoes, tomato purée and 300ml water, and season to taste. Bring to the boil, then reduce the heat and simmer, partially covered, for 25 minutes.

3   Melt the spread in a pan over a medium heat. Add the flour and stir until combined. Cook for 1 minute, stirring continuously. Remove from the heat and add a splash of the milk to create a loose paste, then gradually add the rest of the milk, whisking constantly. Return to a low heat and continue whisking for 2-3 minutes until the sauce is smooth and thickened. Remove from the heat and whisk in the ricotta and nutmeg. Season to taste.

4   Preheat the oven to 200°C, fan 180°C, gas mark 6. Mist a 2-litre baking dish with cooking spray. Spread half the turkey ragù over the bottom of the dish. Cover with a single layer of lasagna sheets (you may need to break them to fit), then spread with half of the ricotta sauce and top with half of the mozzarella. Repeat with the remaining ragù, pasta, sauce and mozzarella, then sprinkle over the grated Parmesan.

5   Cover with foil and bake for 20 minutes. Remove the foil and bake for another 25 minutes in the top of the oven. Set aside to cool for 15 minutes, then serve garnished with the fresh basil, with the salad leaves on the side.

The lasagne can be frozen in an airtight container for up to 3 months.

7 **SmartPoints value per serving**

Gammon, egg & butternut squash chips

serves 4   prep time 5 minutes   cook time 35 minutes

Use ready-cut butternut squash chips to make this tasty meal really quick and simple – nowadays you can find them in most of the big supermarkets.

2 x 300g packs ready-cut butternut squash chips

Calorie controlled cooking spray

2 teaspoons dried mixed herbs

1 tablespoon wholegrain mustard

2 teaspoons clear honey

4 x 200g smoked rindless gammon steaks

1 teaspoon white wine vinegar

4 eggs

70g rocket

1   Preheat the oven to 220°C, fan 200°C, gas mark 7. Put the butternut squash chips in a large food bag, mist the inside with cooking spray and add the mixed herbs. Seal the bag and toss until the chips are coated. Spread them out onto a large baking sheet and bake for 30-35 minutes or until cooked through.

2   Meanwhile, heat the grill to medium. Combine the mustard and honey in a small jug. Brush the gammon steaks with the honey and mustard mixture and cook under the grill for 10 minutes, turning halfway through, until the gammon is golden.

3   While the gammon is cooking, bring a pan of water to a simmer and add the vinegar. Crack an egg onto a saucer, stir the water to create a mini whirlpool, then carefully tip the egg into the centre of the whirlpool. Cook for 3-4 minutes, or until the white of the egg is set, then lift out with a slotted spoon and drain it on kitchen paper. Repeat with the remaining eggs.

4   Serve the poached eggs on top of the grilled gammon with the butternut squash chips and rocket on the side.

Cook's tip
If you can't find ready-cut butternut squash chips, use a whole medium butternut squash, peeled and deseeded, and cut it into 1cm thick chips.

 7   **SmartPoints value per serving**

Chicken Kiev

serves 4   prep time 15 minutes + freezing   cook time 35 minutes

Tender chicken breast fillets are wrapped around a delicious soft cheese, garlic and fresh herb filling, then coated in breadcrumbs and baked.

150g low-fat soft cheese

2 garlic cloves

Small handful fresh parsley, finely chopped

4 skinless chicken breast fillets

25g plain flour

1 egg, lightly beaten

75g dried golden breadcrumbs

Calorie controlled cooking spray

600g new potatoes, halved if large

350g broccoli, cut into florets

1   Put the soft cheese and garlic in a food processor and blitz until smooth. Add the parsley to the food processor and pulse until just combined. Line a small shallow bowl with clingfilm and transfer the mixture to the bowl. Cover and freeze for 2 hours or until solid.

2   Preheat the oven to 200°C, fan 180°C, gas mark 6. Make a large cut in the side of each chicken fillet to create a pocket. Remove the soft cheese from the freezer and cut into 4 pieces. Put 1 piece into the pocket of each chicken fillet, making sure the filling is completely enclosed by the chicken.

3   Put the flour, egg and breadcrumbs into three separate shallow bowls. Dip each chicken breast in the flour, then the egg and then the breadcrumbs. Transfer to a nonstick baking sheet.

4   Mist the chicken fillets with cooking spray, then bake for 30-35 minutes or until the chicken is cooked through.

5   Meanwhile, cook the new potatoes in a pan of boiling water for 10 minutes. Add the broccoli and cook for a further 4-5 minutes, until just tender. Drain and serve the potatoes and broccoli with the chicken.

7 **SmartPoints value per serving**

Pasta Bolognese

serves 4   freezable   prep time 15 minutes   cook time 50 minutes

Who doesn't love a bowl of Bolognese? This classic sauce is simple to make and freezes really well. Serve it with any sort of pasta you like – here, we've used linguine.

Calorie controlled cooking spray
1 onion, finely diced
1 carrot, finely diced
1 celery stick, finely diced
2 teaspoons fennel seeds
400g 5% fat extra lean beef mince
2 garlic cloves, minced
2 x 400g tins chopped tomatoes
1 tablespoon tomato purée
2 teaspoons dried oregano
2 bay leaves
1 beef stock cube
240g linguine pasta
20g Parmesan cheese, grated, to serve
Small handful fresh basil leaves, to garnish

1   Mist a pan with cooking spray and put over a medium heat. Add the onion, carrot, celery and fennel seeds and cook for 6-8 minutes until the vegetables are soft.

2   Add the beef mince and cook for 5 minutes or until it is brown all over. Add the garlic and cook for 1 minute, then add the tomatoes, tomato purée, dried oregano and bay leaves. Crumble in the stock cube and add 375ml water. Bring to a boil, then reduce to a gentle simmer. Cover and cook for 40 minutes until you have a rich, thick sauce. Season to taste.

3   Meanwhile, cook the linguine in a pan of boiling water to pack instructions. Drain and serve with the Bolognese sauce, with the Parmesan cheese and basil leaves scattered over.

The Bolognese sauce can be frozen without the pasta in an airtight container for up to 3 months.

9   **SmartPoints value per serving**

Cook's tip
Want a flavour boost? Swap 125ml of the water for red wine, for an extra 1 SmartPoint per serving.

Chilli con carne

serves 4   freezable   prep time 15 minutes   cook time 40 minutes

A brilliant winter warmer – just leave it to bubble away on the hob for the flavours to develop. The cocoa powder adds depth and richness to the chilli.

Calorie controlled cooking spray

500g 5% fat extra lean
beef mince

1 onion, finely diced

2 garlic cloves, minced

1 tablespoon mild chilli powder

2 teaspoons ground cumin

1 tablespoon plain flour

400ml beef stock, made with
1 stock cube

400g tin chopped tomatoes

400g tin kidney beans,
drained and rinsed

1 tablespoon tomato purée

2 teaspoons cocoa powder

1 teaspoon dried oregano

1 bay leaf

200g brown basmati rice

4 corn cobettes

1 tablespoon chopped
fresh coriander, to garnish

1   Mist a large nonstick pan with cooking spray and put over a medium heat, then add the mince and onion. Cook for 5 minutes, until the beef is brown all over.

2   Add the garlic, chilli powder and cumin and cook for 1 minute. Sprinkle over the flour and stir well.

3   Add the stock, tomatoes, kidney beans, tomato purée, cocoa powder, oregano and bay leaf. Stir well and season to taste. Reduce the heat to a simmer and cover partially with a lid. Leave to cook, stirring occasionally, for 30 minutes until the sauce has thickened.

4   Meanwhile, cook the rice according to pack instructions, and cook the corn cobettes in a pan of simmering water for 5 minutes, or until just tender.

5   Serve the chilli con carne with the rice and corn, garnished with the chopped coriander.

The chilli can be frozen without the rice in an airtight container for up to 3 months.

9   **SmartPoints value per serving**

Cook's tip
Want it spicier? Swap the mild chilli powder for 2 teaspoons of hot chilli powder.

Smoky sausage & bean stew

serves 4   freezable   prep time 15 minutes   cook time 40 minutes

A hearty bangers and bean dish that's so simple to make. Serve it with a side of mash and plenty of fresh parsley for an added flavour boost.

Calorie controlled cooking spray
8 reduced-fat pork sausages
2 red peppers, deseeded and sliced
80g diced chorizo
2 garlic cloves, finely chopped
1 teaspoon smoked paprika
2 x 400g tins chopped tomatoes
2 x 400g tins cannellini beans, drained and rinsed
600g Maris Piper potatoes, quartered
75ml skimmed milk
10g low-fat spread
2 tablespoons finely chopped fresh flat-leaf parsley, to garnish

1   Mist a large nonstick frying pan with cooking spray and put over a medium-high heat. Add the sausages and cook for 6-8 minutes, turning regularly, until browned on all sides. Remove from the pan and set aside.

2   Add the peppers to the pan and cook for 4-5 minutes until softened, then add the chorizo and cook for a further 2 minutes until it starts to release its oil.

3   Add the garlic and paprika and cook for a further 2 minutes, then add the tomatoes and 200ml water. Stir to combine and season to taste.

4   Return the sausages to the pan and simmer for 10 minutes. Stir in the beans and cook for 2 minutes until heated through.

5   Meanwhile, cook the potatoes in a pan of boiling water for 10-12 minutes until tender. Drain and mash with the skimmed milk and low-fat spread. Season to taste.

6   Serve the stew garnished with the fresh parsley, with the mashed potatoes on the side.

The stew can be frozen in an airtight container for up to 3 months.

10 **SmartPoints value per serving**

Moussaka

serves 6   freezable   prep time 25 minutes   cook time 1 hour 20 minutes

Rekindle memories of holidays in Greece with this classic all-in-one dish of lamb mince, aubergines and potatoes, with a yogurt and feta topping.

2 aubergines, trimmed and cut into 1cm-thick rounds
Calorie controlled cooking spray
1 large onion, finely chopped
2 garlic cloves, crushed
500g 10% fat lamb mince
2 tablespoons tomato purée
¾ teaspoon ground cinnamon
400g tin chopped tomatoes
2 teaspoons dried oregano
150g 0% fat natural Greek yogurt
1 egg, beaten
30g grated Parmesan
30g light feta cheese, crumbled
70g rocket

1 Preheat the oven to 190°C, fan 170°C, gas mark 5 and line 2 large baking sheets with baking paper. Spread the aubergine slices out on the baking sheets, then cook for 15 minutes. Remove from the oven and set aside, leaving the oven on.

2 Meanwhile, mist a large pan with cooking spray and put over a medium heat. Add the onion and garlic and cook, stirring, for 6-8 minutes, until soft. Add the lamb mince and cook, stirring, for 5 minutes, until brown all over. Drain off any excess fat from the pan.

3 Add the tomato purée and cinnamon to the pan and cook, stirring, for 1 minute. Add the chopped tomatoes and the oregano, along with 200ml water, and season to taste. Bring to the boil, then reduce the heat and simmer, stirring occasionally, for 15 minutes.

4 Whisk the yogurt, egg, half of the Parmesan and half of the feta cheese together in a bowl until combined. Spread half the lamb mixture in a 2-litre baking dish. Arrange half the aubergine slices in a single layer on top. Top with another layer of lamb followed by the remaining aubergine. Spoon over the yogurt mixture and scatter with the remaining Parmesan and feta cheese. Bake for 35 minutes or until golden, then serve with the rocket.

The moussaka can be frozen in an airtight container for up to 3 months.

5 **SmartPoints value per serving**

Baked potato toppings

Baked potatoes are a brilliant base for all kinds of tasty toppings – here are some easy ideas to transform a humble jacket spud into something really special.

To bake the potatoes

Preheat the oven to 220°C, fan 200°C, gas mark 7. Prick 4 x 180g **baking potatoes** with a fork, then mist with **calorie controlled cooking spray** and rub with **salt**. Bake directly on the oven shelf for 20 minutes. Reduce the temperature to 190°C, fan 170°C, gas mark 5 and bake for 1 hour or until the potatoes are tender and the skin is crisp and golden.

Tuna melt

serves 4   prep time 15 minutes
cook time 1 hour 30 minutes

Bake 4 x 180g **baking potatoes** as above. Reduce the oven temperature to 180°C, fan 160°C, gas mark 4. Drain 3 x 160g tins **tuna in spring water** and put in a bowl with 4 trimmed and chopped **spring onions**, 2 tablespoons chopped **fresh chives**, 2 tablespoons **reduced-fat mayonnaise** and 20g grated **half-fat Cheddar cheese**. Halve the potatoes and scoop out the flesh into a second bowl, leaving a 1cm shell. Put the shells on a baking sheet. Mash the scooped out potato and add to the tuna mixture. Season to taste and stir to combine, then spoon into the potato shells. Sprinkle over another 20g grated **half-fat Cheddar cheese** and bake for 10 minutes until golden, then serve.

9 SmartPoints value per serving

Smoky bean

serves 4   prep time 15 minutes
cook time 1 hour 20 minutes

Bake 4 x 180g **baking potatoes** as above. While they're cooking, mist a pan with **calorie controlled cooking spray** and put over a medium heat. Add 1 thinly sliced **red onion** and 1 deseeded, sliced **red pepper**, and cook for 6-8 minutes until soft. Add 2 chopped **garlic cloves**, a 400g tin **chopped tomatoes**, 1 teaspoon **smoked paprika**, 2 teaspoons **red wine vinegar**, 1 teaspoon **clear honey** and 2 x 400g tins drained and rinsed **butter beans**. Bring to a simmer and cook for 10-15 minutes or until the sauce has reduced. Make a cut in the baked potatoes and open them out slightly. Top each one with the beans and scatter over some chopped **fresh flat-leaf parsley**, then serve.

8 SmartPoints value per serving

BLT

serves 4   prep time 10 minutes
cook time 1 hour 20 minutes

Bake 4 x 180g **baking potatoes** as above. Mist a large pan with **calorie controlled cooking spray** and put over a medium heat. Add 6 **bacon medallions** and cook for 2-3 minutes on each side until golden. Remove from the pan and roughly chop. Meanwhile, in a small bowl whisk together 120ml **buttermilk** and 40g **reduced-fat mayonnaise**, then season to taste. Make a cut in the baked potatoes and open them out slightly. Season to taste, then top with 12 quartered **cherry tomatoes** and the bacon. Garnish with shredded **iceberg lettuce**, then drizzle over the buttermilk dressing and serve.

9 SmartPoints value per serving

Cheese & ham souffle

serves 4   prep time 15 minutes
cook time 1 hour 30 minutes

Bake 4 x 180g **baking potatoes** as above and set aside until cool enough to handle. Reduce the oven temperature to 180°C, fan 160°C, gas mark 4. Halve the potatoes and scoop out the flesh into a mixing bowl, leaving a 1cm shell. Put the shells on a baking sheet. Mash the potato with a fork, then add 100g roughly chopped **wafer thin ham**, 2 **egg yolks**, 2 tablespoons chopped **fresh flat-leaf parsley**, 2 tablespoons **skimmed milk** and 1 teaspoon **Dijon mustard**. Mix until well combined. In a separate bowl, whisk 2 **egg whites** until light and fluffy. Fold the egg whites into the potato mixture and spoon it into the potato shells. Top with 40g grated **half-fat Cheddar cheese** and bake for 6-8 minutes until golden, then serve.

9 SmartPoints value per serving

Vegetarian

Quorn & lentil cottage pie

serves 4   prep time 15 minutes   cook time 1 hour 25 minutes

This veggie version of the much-loved classic has a tasty filling made with lentils and Quorn. A little bit of Marmite added to the filling gives it a rich, savoury flavour.

110g dried Puy lentils
1 vegetable stock cube, crumbled
600g potatoes, peeled and chopped
2 tablespoons skimmed milk
60g half-fat mature Cheddar, grated
2 teaspoons vegetable oil
1 large onion, chopped
1 carrot, diced
2 celery sticks, chopped
2 garlic cloves, chopped
200g Quorn mince
2 teaspoons dried mixed herbs
**4 teaspoons vegetable
gravy granules**
½ tablespoon Marmite yeast extract
320g Tenderstem broccoli, to serve

1   Rinse and drain the lentils, then put them in a pan with 400ml water. Cover and simmer for 30 minutes until the lentils are tender and most of the water has been absorbed. Stir in the stock cube until dissolved, adding a splash more water if needed.

2   Meanwhile, bring a second pan of water to the boil, add the potatoes and cook for 15 minutes until tender. Drain and mash well with the milk and half the cheese, then season to taste.

3   Preheat the oven to 200°C, fan 180°C, gas mark 6. Heat the oil in a large frying pan, add the onion, carrot, and celery and cook slowly for 15 minutes or until softened.

4   Add the garlic and cook for 2 minutes, then stir in the Quorn, herbs, gravy granules, Marmite and 250ml hot water. Stir in the lentils, bring to the boil, then spoon the mixture into a 1.2 litre ovenproof dish. Top with the mash, using a fork to gently spread to the edges. Scatter over the remaining cheese and bake for 30-40 minutes until golden.

5   Just before the end of the cooking time, cook the broccoli in a pan of boiling water for 3-4 minutes, or until just tender. Serve with the cottage pie.

7 SmartPoints value per serving

Bubble & squeak cakes with fried eggs

serves 4   freezable   prep time 20 minutes   cook time 40 minutes

Traditionally a way to use up leftovers from the Sunday roast, these little veggie cakes topped with a fried egg are great for a quick breakfast or brunch.

500g Maris Piper potatoes, cut into small chunks
150g Brussels sprouts, shredded
100g Savoy cabbage, shredded
¼ teaspoon ground nutmeg
20g plain flour
Calorie controlled cooking spray
2 shallots, finely chopped
450g young leaf spinach
4 eggs

1   Bring a large pan of water to the boil over a medium heat and cook the potatoes for 15-20 minutes until tender, adding the sprouts and cabbage for the last 3 minutes. Drain and return to the pan to steam-dry for a couple of minutes.

2   Add the nutmeg, then mash until the potatoes are smooth and the vegetables have broken up a bit. Season to taste. Allow to cool slightly, then shape the mixture into 8 patties.

3   Preheat the oven to 120°C, fan 100°C, gas mark ½. Put the flour onto a large plate and lightly coat the patties in the flour. Mist a large frying pan with cooking spray and cook the patties over a medium heat for 4-5 minutes on each side until golden, then transfer to a baking sheet and put in the oven to keep warm.

4   Wipe the pan clean and mist with cooking spray. Add the shallots and cook for 3 minutes or until soft, adding a splash of water if it gets dry. Add the spinach and cook, stirring, for 2 minutes until the spinach has wilted – you may need to add the spinach in 2 batches. Season to taste. Transfer to a bowl, cover and keep warm.

Cook's tip
You can freeze the bubble & squeak cakes for up to 3 months.

5   Wipe the pan, mist with cooking spray again and fry the eggs for 2-3 minutes until the whites have set. Serve the cakes with the spinach on the side and a fried egg on top with a sprinkling of freshly ground black pepper.

4 SmartPoints value per serving

Garlic cauliflower steaks with roast veg

serves 4**prep time 15 minutes****cook time 40 minutes**

Fancy a Sunday roast but don't want to eat meat? Transform cauliflower from a simple side dish to star of the show with this easy idea for a veggie roast dinner.

3 tablespoons low-fat spread

2 garlic cloves, crushed

2 tablespoons finely chopped fresh flat-leaf parsley, plus extra to serve

Grated zest of ½ lemon

Large pinch chilli powder, plus extra to garnish

1 whole cauliflower, leaves removed

600g potatoes, cut into 3cm cubes

Calorie controlled cooking spray

300g Tenderstem broccoli

300g mixed cherry tomatoes, halved

1   Preheat the oven to 200°C, fan 180°C, gas mark 6. Mix the spread, garlic, parsley, lemon zest and chilli together in a small bowl until well combined and season well. Cut the cauliflower into 4 thick steaks and rub the spread all over them, then set aside.

2   Put the potatoes in a single layer in a large roasting tin, mist with cooking spray and season to taste. Cook for 20 minutes, then add the broccoli and tomatoes, mist with more cooking spray and cook for a further 20 minutes.

3   Meanwhile, put a large griddle pan over a medium heat. When hot, add the cauliflower steaks and cook for 10-15 minutes, turning once or twice, until tender and slightly charred – you may need to do this in batches. Serve with the roasted vegetables, garnished with the extra chopped parsley and a sprinkling of chilli powder.

 5 SmartPoints value per serving

Cook's tip
To cut the cauliflower into steaks, put it base-down on a cutting board, then cut through the middle into 2 halves. Cut each half into 2 thick slices – you could use any trimmings in a soup or salad.

French onion risotto

serves 4 **prep time 10 minutes** **cook time 55 minutes**

Creamy, flavoursome risotto is hard to beat for a really satisfying, all-in-one meal. If you've never made it before, try this simple recipe with onions, garlic and parsley.

Calorie controlled cooking spray
3 large onions, finely sliced
1 garlic clove, finely chopped
250g Arborio rice
1.2 litres hot vegetable stock, made using 1½ stock cubes
2 tablespoons grated vegetarian Italian hard cheese
1 tablespoon finely chopped fresh flat-leaf parsley, plus extra to serve

1   Mist a large pan with cooking spray and cook the onions over a medium heat for 5 minutes, then cover the pan with the lid and cook for another 20-25 minutes, stirring occasionally, until caramelised. Add the garlic and cook for another minute.

2   Remove half of the onions from the pan and set aside. Add the rice to the pan with the remaining onions and cook, stirring, for 2 minutes.

3   Add a ladle of stock to the pan and stir occasionally until the rice has absorbed almost all of the stock. Repeat until all the stock has been used and the rice is just tender – this will take about 20 minutes (see Cook's tip).

4   Stir in most of the cheese, the chopped parsley and the reserved onions, then season to taste. Scatter over the extra parsley, the remaining cheese and some freshly ground black pepper, then serve.

 8 **SmartPoints value per serving**

Cook's tip
You may not need to use all the stock – stop adding it when the rice is just tender.

Spanish omelette

serves 4   prep time 15 minutes   cook time 50 minutes

A really easy potato, onion and red pepper omelette that makes a meal in itself.
It's delicious served hot, but just as good eaten cold for lunch the next day.

400g waxy potatoes, cut into 3mm slices
Calorie controlled cooking spray
2 onions, thinly sliced
1 red pepper, thinly sliced
9 eggs, beaten
Small handful fresh flat-leaf parsley

FOR THE SALAD
2 teaspoons olive oil
1 teaspoon balsamic vinegar
1 teaspoon lemon juice
100g rocket
250g cherry tomatoes, halved
½ cucumber, cut into ribbons with a vegetable peeler

1 Put the potatoes in a pan and pour over boiling water until just covered. Bring to a simmer, then cover and cook for 15 minutes or until just tender, then drain and set aside.

2 Preheat the grill to medium. Mist a 23cm nonstick ovenproof frying pan with cooking spray and cook the onions for 6-8 minutes until soft, then add the pepper and cook for another 5 minutes.

3 Mist the pan again with cooking spray and add the potatoes to the onions and pepper. Season to taste, then pour in the eggs and cook over a medium-low heat for 10-15 minutes or until most of the egg has set – you should just be able to lift the bottom of the omelette up with a spatula. Transfer the pan to the grill and cook for a further 3-4 minutes until the top of the omelette has set. Leave to cool for 5 minutes.

4 Meanwhile, mix the olive oil, balsamic vinegar and lemon juice together in a small jug until well combined, then toss with the rocket, tomatoes and cucumber in a serving bowl.

5 Scatter the parsley over the omelette, then slice into wedges and serve with the salad.

3 **SmartPoints value per serving**

Cook's tip
Be sure to use the best nonstick pan you have, it'll make a big difference when you're turning the omelette out onto the plate and it'll stop the outside from going too brown.

Red lentil & butternut squash dhal

serves 4   freezable   prep time 15 minutes   cook time 40 minutes

Budget-friendly, colourful and full of flavour, this satisfying lentil curry is great for batch cooking – why not make double and freeze half for another time?

Calorie controlled cooking spray
2 red onions, halved and sliced
2 tablespoons mild curry powder
3cm piece fresh ginger, grated
600g butternut squash, peeled, deseeded and cut into 3cm cubes
2 tablespoons tomato purée
1.2 litres hot vegetable stock, made with 1½ stock cubes
300g red lentils
Handful fresh coriander, leaves picked and stalks finely chopped
Juice of ½ lime
240g brown basmati rice
1 small red chilli, finely sliced

1   Mist a large, heavy-based pan with cooking spray and cook the onions over a medium heat for 6-8 minutes until soft. Add the curry powder, ginger, squash and tomato purée and cook, stirring, for 2 minutes.

2   Add the stock, lentils and coriander stalks, then cover and gently simmer for 25-30 minutes, until the vegetables are tender. Season to taste and stir in the lime juice, then allow the dhal to stand, uncovered, for 5-10 minutes to absorb any excess liquid before serving.

3   Meanwhile, cook the rice to pack instructions.

4   Scatter the coriander leaves and sliced chilli over the dhal, then serve with the rice.

The dhal can be frozen in an airtight container for up to 3 months.

7   **SmartPoints value per serving**

Cook's tip
In a hurry? Save time by using ready-prepared butternut squash.

Mushroom stroganoff

serves 4   **prep time 15 minutes**   **cook time 20 minutes**

Creamy and rich, this luxurious looking dish is surprisingly quick and easy to make. This veggie version is packed with flavour, with a little chilli powder giving it a hint of heat.

Calorie controlled cooking spray
1 large onion, finely chopped
½ tablespoon paprika
¼ teaspoon chilli powder
2 garlic cloves, crushed
600g button mushrooms, sliced
80g low-fat soft cheese
**2 tablespoons fat-free
natural yogurt**
**2 tablespoons finely chopped fresh
flat-leaf parsley, plus extra
chopped leaves, to serve**
**2 x 250g pouches microwave
brown basmati rice**

1 Mist a large frying pan with cooking spray and cook the onion for 6-8 minutes over a medium heat until soft, then add the spices and garlic and cook for another minute. Add the mushrooms and cook for 7-8 minutes, or until tender.

2 Stir in the soft cheese and yogurt and allow to melt, then stir in the chopped parsley and season to taste.

3 Cook the rice to pack instructions. Serve the stroganoff with the rice and an extra scattering of parsley.

  SmartPoints value per serving

Roasted tomato soup with cheese toasties

serves 4   freezable   prep time 15 minutes   cook time 1 hour 5 minutes

When it's blowing a gale outside, what could be better than a big bowl of delicious tomato soup? One that's served with a cheese toastie on the side, of course!

½ red onion, cut into thin wedges

800g vine tomatoes, halved

3 garlic cloves, thickly sliced

½ tablespoon olive oil

300ml hot vegetable stock, made with 1 stock cube

2 tablespoons finely chopped fresh basil, plus extra leaves, to garnish

4 slices Weight Watchers Soft Malted Danish Bread

2 teaspoons Marmite yeast extract

100g half-fat Cheddar cheese, grated

1   Preheat the oven to 160°C, fan 140°C, gas mark 3. Put the onion, tomatoes (cut-side up) and garlic onto a baking sheet lined with baking paper. Drizzle with the oil and season to taste. Roast for 1 hour until all the vegetables are soft. Remove from the oven and increase the temperature to 180°C, fan 160°C, gas mark 4.

2   Put the roasted vegetables and garlic, along with any juices, into a blender with the stock and basil, and blend until smooth. Keep warm in a pan while you make the toasties.

3   Lightly toast the bread, then spread two of the slices with the Marmite, followed by three-quarters of the grated cheese. Put the other pieces of toast on top and scatter over the remaining cheese, then put both sandwiches onto a baking sheet and bake for 2-3 minutes until the cheese is golden and melted. Cut into triangles, then serve the soup with an extra scattering of basil leaves, a sprinkling of freshly ground black pepper and the toasties on the side.

The soup can be frozen in an airtight container for up to 6 months.

Cook's tip
This soup is also just as delicious served cold.

4   SmartPoints value per serving

Ratatouille

serves 4   **prep time 20 minutes**   **cook time 35 minutes**

This classic French vegetable stew is a real feast for the eyes! It's a simple yet delicious dish, packed with flavour and colour.

Calorie controlled cooking spray

1 large onion, finely chopped

2 large aubergines, trimmed and cut into 3cm pieces

2 large courgettes, trimmed and cut into 2cm-thick half moons

2 yellow peppers, deseeded and cut into 3cm pieces

2 garlic cloves, finely chopped

2 large tomatoes, quartered

400g tin chopped tomatoes

2 tablespoons finely chopped fresh basil, plus extra leaves to garnish

½ tablespoon fresh thyme leaves, roughly chopped, plus extra sprigs, to garnish

Finely grated zest of 1 lemon

4 x 65g crusty white bread rolls, to serve

1. Mist a large lidded pan with cooking spray and put over a high heat. Add the onion, aubergines, courgettes and peppers, then cook for 10 minutes until browned. You may need to do this in batches.

2. Add the garlic and cook for another minute, then add the fresh and tinned tomatoes. Cover and gently simmer for 20 minutes, stirring occasionally until the vegetables are tender but not breaking up.

3. Season to taste and stir in the chopped basil, thyme and lemon zest. Garnish with the extra basil leaves and thyme sprigs, then serve with the bread rolls.

5 **SmartPoints value per serving**

Cook's tip

Try serving this without the bread as a great zero SmartPoints side dish.

Lentil hash with poached eggs

serves 4   prep time 15 minutes   cook time 20 minutes

Turn a tin of lentils into a satisfying meal with a few tasty additions. Top with a poached egg and you have the perfect dish for brunch or a quick lunch.

300g potatoes, cut into 2cm pieces
Calorie controlled cooking spray
1 large onion, finely sliced
2 garlic cloves, finely chopped
2 teaspoons ground cumin
2 teaspoons ground coriander
2 x 400g tins green lentils, drained and rinsed
200g cherry tomatoes, halved
100g young leaf spinach
1 teaspoon white wine vinegar
4 eggs
Small handful fresh flat-leaf parsley, leaves picked
Pinch of mild chilli powder, to serve

1 Cook the potatoes in a pan of boiling water for 8-10 minutes until just tender, then drain and let stand, uncovered for 2 minutes to dry.

2 Mist a large frying pan with cooking spray and cook the onion over a medium heat for 6-8 minutes until soft, then add the garlic, cumin and coriander, and cook for 1 minute. Add the potatoes to the pan and cook for 5-6 minutes until golden, then stir in the lentils, tomatoes and spinach and season to taste. Cook over a low heat for 10 minutes.

3 Meanwhile, bring a pan of water to a simmer and add the vinegar. Crack an egg onto a saucer, then stir the simmering water to create a mini whirlpool. Carefully tip the egg into the centre of the whirlpool. Cook for 3-4 minutes, or until the egg white is set, then lift out with a slotted spoon and drain on kitchen paper. Repeat with the remaining eggs.

4 Serve the hash with the poached eggs on top, with a scattering of parsley leaves and a sprinkling of chilli powder and black pepper.

2 SmartPoints value per serving

Cook's tip
If you fancy a change, swap the lentils for chickpeas – the SmartPoints will be the same.

Veggie lasagne

serves 4   freezable   prep time 20 minutes   cook time 1 hour 10 minutes

This delicious veggie lasagne is really easy to put together. The vegetables in the filling are roasted for maximum flavour.

1 onion, finely chopped

2 garlic cloves, still in their skin and lightly crushed

2 aubergines, trimmed and cut into 3cm chunks

400g mushrooms, thickly sliced

Calorie controlled cooking spray

500g passata

6 dried lasagna sheets

100g half-fat crème fraîche

2 tablespoons vegetarian Italian hard cheese, grated

4 vine tomatoes, sliced, to serve

Salad leaves, to serve

1   Preheat the oven to 200°C, fan 180°C, gas mark 4. Put the onion, garlic, aubergines and mushrooms into a large roasting tin, mist with cooking spray and season well. Roast for 30-40 minutes until golden and tender. Cool slightly, then squeeze the garlic out of their skins, roughly chop and toss back in with the vegetables.

2   Mist a deep 20cm square baking dish with cooking spray and spoon in enough of the vegetables to cover the bottom. Pour over a little passata and top with a layer of lasagna sheets. Repeat until you have used up all the vegetables, passata and pasta, finishing with a layer of pasta.

3   Dollop over the crème fraîche, season to taste and sprinkle over the grated cheese.

4   Bake for 30 minutes until the top is golden, then serve with the sliced vine tomatoes and salad leaves on the side.

The lasagne can be frozen in an airtight container for up to 2 months.

6   **SmartPoints value per serving**

Cook's tip
To reduce the SmartPoints, replace the pasta with thin slices of butternut squash for a total of 3 SmartPoints per serving.

Creamy spinach & mushroom gnocchi

serves 4   **prep time 10 minutes**   **cook time 15 minutes**

We've teamed these little potato dumplings with a creamy spinach sauce – the whole dish is on the table in under 30 minutes.

400g gnocchi
Calorie controlled cooking spray
1 onion, finely chopped
1 garlic clove, crushed
200g young leaf spinach
Grated zest and juice of 1 lemon
125g half-fat crème fraîche
1 tablespoon finely chopped fresh flat-leaf parsley
1 courgette, trimmed and sliced into ribbons with a vegetable peeler

1   Cook the gnocchi in a pan of boiling water to pack instructions, then drain.

2   Meanwhile, mist a pan with cooking spray and put over a medium heat. Add the onion, along with 1 tablespoon of water, then cover and cook for 6-8 minutes until soft. Add the garlic and cook, uncovered, for another minute.

3   Add the spinach and stir until wilted, then add the lemon zest, crème fraîche and parsley, stirring well to combine. Season to taste, then add the gnocchi and stir well until they are coated in the sauce.

4   Put the courgette ribbons in a serving bowl and toss with the lemon juice, then season to taste. Serve the gnocchi with the courgette salad.

7 **SmartPoints value per serving**

Cauliflower curry

serves 4   prep time 20 minutes   cook time 40 minutes

Try this easy veggie curry with a tomato-based sauce – you can add more spices if you want to dial up the flavour.

Calorie controlled cooking spray
1 large onion, finely chopped
3cm piece fresh ginger, grated
2 garlic cloves, crushed
½ teaspoon ground turmeric
1½ teaspoons ground cumin
2 teaspoons mild curry powder
400g tin chopped tomatoes
1 large cauliflower, cut into florets
200g tomatoes, quartered
60g frozen garden peas
Juice of ½ lime
2 x 250g pouches microwave brown basmati rice
2 tablespoons fat-free natural yogurt, to serve
2 tablespoons finely chopped coriander, to garnish

1   Mist a large lidded pan with cooking spray and cook the onion over a medium heat for 6-8 minutes until soft, then add the ginger, garlic, turmeric, cumin and curry powder, and cook for another 2 minutes, stirring constantly.

2   Tip in the chopped tomatoes and cauliflower and season to taste. Put the lid on and gently simmer for 25-30 minutes until the cauliflower is tender, stirring occasionally. Add the fresh tomatoes and peas during the last 3-4 minutes of the cooking time, then stir in the lime juice.

3   Cook the rice to pack instructions, and serve the curry on a bed of rice with a dollop of natural yogurt and a scattering of fresh coriander.

6 SmartPoints value per serving

Veggie meatballs with carrot 'spaghetti'

serves 4   **prep time 40 minutes**   **cook time 40 minutes**

Our meat-free version of spaghetti and meatballs is a winner! These chickpea and mushroom meatballs with carrot noodles taste amazing – and all for just 1 SmartPoint.

400g tin chickpeas

300g mushrooms, roughly chopped

Calorie controlled cooking spray

3 garlic cloves, crushed

1 tablespoon dried oregano

2 tablespoons finely chopped fresh flat-leaf parsley, plus extra leaves, to garnish

½ tablespoon finely chopped chives

30g dried breadcrumbs

2 x 400g tins chopped tomatoes

600g carrots, peeled and spiralised

1 Preheat the oven to 200°C, fan 180°C, gas mark 6 and line a baking sheet with baking paper. Drain the chickpeas but reserve the liquid and set aside. Blitz the mushrooms in a food processor until very finely chopped.

2 Mist a frying pan with cooking spray and cook the mushrooms over a high heat for 5 minutes until tender and most of the water has evaporated, then add half the garlic, the oregano, half of the parsley and all of the chives, and cook for another 2 minutes.

3 Put the chickpeas in a food processor and blitz to a purée, then add to the pan and season to taste. Stir in the breadcrumbs and 50ml chickpea water so the mixture comes together. Allow to cool slightly, then shape the mixture into 12 balls, put them onto the lined baking sheet and mist with cooking spray. Bake for 25 minutes until golden.

4 Meanwhile, mist a pan with cooking spray and fry the remaining garlic for 1 minute, then add the chopped tomatoes. Season to taste and simmer for 15 minutes, then stir in the remaining parsley. When the meatballs are done, add them to the sauce and stir to coat

5 Mist another frying pan with cooking spray and cook the spiralised carrots for 4-5 minutes until just tender. Serve with the meatballs and a scattering of extra parsley leaves over the top.

Cook's tip
Swap the spiralised carrots for 240g wholewheat spaghetti. The SmartPoints will be 6 per serving.

1   SmartPoints value per serving

Mac 'n' cheese

serves 4   freezable   prep time 20 minutes   cook time 45 minutes

This easy, cheesy pasta bake will be a favourite with all the family and makes a great treat when the weather turns cooler. A pinch of cayenne pepper adds a spicy kick.

260g macaroni
1½ tablespoons plain flour
300ml skimmed milk
25g low-fat spread
100g half-fat Cheddar cheese, grated
1 teaspoon Dijon mustard
Large pinch cayenne pepper
2 tablespoons dried breadcrumbs
200g Tenderstem broccoli, to serve
Fresh flat-leaf parsley, to garnish

1   Preheat the oven to 190°C, fan 170°C, gas mark 5. Cook the macaroni according to pack instructions, then drain.

2   Whisk the flour with 100ml of the milk until smooth. Pour into a pan and gently heat, stirring constantly until it starts to thicken. Gradually add the remaining milk, whisking until smooth, then simmer gently for 2 minutes before removing from the heat.

3   Add the spread to the sauce, along with two-thirds of the cheese, the mustard, cayenne pepper and some freshly ground black pepper. Allow the cheese to melt, then stir to combine. Season to taste.

4   Add the pasta to the sauce and stir until coated, then pour everything into a 20cm baking dish. Combine the remaining cheese with the breadcrumbs and scatter over the pasta, then bake for 25 minutes, or until golden.

5   Meanwhile, cook the broccoli in a pan of boiling water for 5-6 minutes until just tender. Scatter the parsley over the mac 'n' cheese, then serve with the broccoli.

The mac 'n' cheese can be frozen in an airtight container for up to 2 months

Cook's tip
Try adding cubes of roasted butternut squash, for no extra SmartPoints.

12 SmartPoints value per serving

Porridge

Healthy and warming, porridge for breakfast can keep you satisfied until lunch. Keep things interesting with different toppings, like these delicious ideas.

Spiced fruit

serves 4   prep time 5 minutes
cook time 10 minutes

Put 250g frozen **summer fruits**, the juice of ½ **orange**, 1 **cinnamon stick**, ½ **star anise** and 1 tablespoon **clear honey** in a small pan and place over a medium heat. When it starts to bubble, reduce the heat to low and cook for 10 minutes, using a wooden spoon to stir, until the liquid is reduced and slightly sticky. Meanwhile, put 120g **porridge oats** in a large pan. Add 500ml **skimmed milk** and 250ml water, stir well, then put over a medium heat and bring to the boil. Reduce the heat, and simmer for 3-4 minutes, stirring continuously, until thick and creamy. Discard the cinnamon stick and star anise and serve the compote with the porridge.

 6   SmartPoints value per serving

Tropical bliss

serves 4   prep time 5 minutes
cook time 10 minutes

Put 120g **porridge oats** in a large pan. Add 500ml **Alpro Coconut Drink** and 250ml water, stir well, then put over a medium heat and bring to the boil. Reduce the heat and simmer for 3-4 minutes, stirring continuously, until thick and creamy. Meanwhile, toast 2 tablespoons **coconut flakes** in a dry, nonstick frying pan over a medium heat for 1 minute, until golden and fragrant. Divide the porridge between 4 bowls and top with 1 **mango**, cut into chunks, the pulp of 2 **passion fruit** and the coconut flakes.

 7   SmartPoints value per serving

Banana & hazelnut

serves 4   prep time 10 minutes
cook time 10 minutes

Put 120g **porridge oats** in a large pan. Add 500ml **skimmed milk** and 250ml water, stir well, then put over a medium heat and bring to the boil. Reduce the heat and simmer for 3-4 minutes, stirring continuously, until thick and creamy. Stir 2 teaspoons **date syrup** into the porridge so it's rippled but not completely combined. Divide the porridge between 4 bowls and top each one with half a sliced **banana** and ¼ teaspoon of chopped **toasted hazelnuts**, then drizzle each bowl with another ½ teaspoon of **date syrup**.

 6   SmartPoints value per serving

Pear & cinnamon

serves 4   prep time 5 minutes
cook time 5 minutes

Put 120g **porridge oats** in a large pan. Add 500ml **skimmed milk**, 250ml of water and 1 teaspoon **ground cinnamon**, stir well, then put over a medium heat and bring to the boil. Reduce the heat, and simmer for 3-4 minutes, stirring continuously, until thick and creamy. Grate 1 large cored **pear**, and stir it into the porridge. Slice another large pear and toss with a squeeze of **lemon juice**. Divide the porridge between 4 bowls and top with the sliced pear, 1 tablespoon **0% fat natural Greek yogurt** per serving and a sprinkling of **cinnamon**.

 5   SmartPoints value per serving

Fakeaways

Fish & chips

serves 4   prep time 20 minutes   cook time 15 minutes

Our favourite fast food gets a healthy makeover with succulent cod fillets baked in a crispy, cheesy breadcrumb coating and served with butternut squash chips and crushed peas.

60g panko breadcrumbs
40g half-fat Cheddar, finely grated
2 tablespoons plain flour
1 egg
4 x 120g skinless cod fillets
Calorie controlled cooking spray
1 butternut squash, peeled, deseeded and cut into chips
2 garlic cloves, left whole
2 teaspoons olive oil
300g frozen peas
4-5 spring onions, trimmed and finely sliced on the diagonal
Handful fresh mint, roughly chopped
1 lemon, cut into wedges, to serve

1   Preheat the oven to 220°C, fan 200°C, gas mark 7. Line a baking sheet with baking paper. In a bowl, combine the breadcrumbs and grated cheese. Put the flour into a second bowl and season to taste. Crack the egg into a third bowl and beat lightly with a fork or whisk. Dust the cod with the flour, then dip in the egg and finally the breadcrumb mixture, turning to coat well. Transfer to the lined baking sheet and mist with cooking spray.

2   Put the butternut squash chips and garlic cloves in a roasting tin, drizzle with the oil and season to taste.

3   Bake the fish and chips for 15 minutes until the fish is cooked through and the chips are tender. Squeeze the garlic from the skins and toss through the chips.

4   Meanwhile, cook the peas in a pan of boiling water for 5 minutes. Drain and return to the pan. Roughly crush, then stir in the sliced spring onions and mint. Season to taste and keep warm until the fish and chips are ready. Serve with the lemon wedges to squeeze over.

Cook's tip
Replace the butternut squash with 600g sweet potatoes, for a total of 9 SmartPoints per serving.

4   **SmartPoints value per serving**

Chicken curry

serves 4   freezable   prep time 10 minutes   cook time 35 minutes

We're a nation of curry lovers, but there's no need to buy it in when you can have this classic chicken curry with coriander rice on the table in just 45 minutes.

Calorie controlled cooking spray
1 onion, finely sliced
2 garlic cloves, crushed
3cm piece fresh ginger, grated
3 tablespoons mild curry powder
650g skinless chicken breast, diced
400g tin chopped tomatoes
200ml chicken stock, made with ½ stock cube
2 x 250g packs microwave brown basmati rice
Juice of ½ lime, plus extra wedges to serve
2 tablespoons roughly chopped fresh coriander, plus extra leaves, to garnish
80g fat-free natural yogurt, to serve
Pinch of garam masala, to serve

1 Mist a large pan with cooking spray, add the onion and cook over a medium heat for 6-8 minutes until soft. Add the garlic and ginger and cook for another minute, then stir in the curry powder and cook for a further 2 minutes.

2 Add the chicken and cook for 2 minutes, stirring to coat in the spice mixture. Add the chopped tomatoes and stock, bring to a simmer and cook for 15-20 minutes until the chicken is cooked through and the sauce has thickened.

3 Cook the rice to pack instructions, then stir in the lime juice and coriander. Serve the curry with the rice and lime wedges to squeeze over. Top with a dollop of yogurt, a sprinkling of garam masala and extra coriander leaves.

The curry can be frozen, without the rice, in an airtight container for up to 3 months.

7   **SmartPoints value per serving**

Cook's tip
Swap the rice for cauliflower rice, for a total of 2 SmartPoints per serving.

Beef & black bean burgers

serves 4   prep time 20 minutes + chilling   cook time 25 minutes

These flavour-packed burgers are served with an easy but delicious coleslaw made with a yogurt and chive dressing.

Calorie controlled cooking spray

5 spring onions, trimmed and roughly chopped

1 garlic clove, finely chopped

1 teaspoon smoked paprika

1 teaspoon ground cumin

475g 5% fat beef mince

2 teaspoons Dijon mustard

150g tinned black beans, drained, rinsed and lightly crushed

2 teaspoons olive oil

4 x 60g wholemeal burger buns

Sliced tomatoes, sliced gherkins, and lettuce leaves, to serve

FOR THE COLESLAW

100g white cabbage, shredded

1 carrot, peeled and grated

100g chargrilled red peppers in brine, drained and thinly sliced

40g 0% fat natural Greek yogurt

1 teaspoon white wine vinegar

2 tablespoons snipped fresh chives

1 Mist a frying pan with cooking spray and put over a medium heat. Add the spring onions and garlic, and cook for 2-3 minutes. Stir in the smoked paprika and cumin, and cook for 1 minute, then transfer to a mixing bowl.

2 Add the mince, mustard and beans to the bowl. Season to taste and combine. Shape into 4 patties, then chill in the fridge for 30 minutes.

3 Put a griddle or frying pan over a medium-high heat, brush the patties with the oil and fry for 3-4 minutes each side. Reduce the heat to low and cook for a further 5 minutes on each side.

4 Meanwhile, make the coleslaw. Put the cabbage, carrot and peppers in a serving bowl. In a separate bowl, whisk together the yogurt, vinegar and chives. Season to taste, then toss the dressing with the vegetables.

5 Top each bun base with tomatoes, gherkins and lettuce, then the burgers, coleslaw and bun top. Serve any extra coleslaw on the side.

8 SmartPoints value per serving

Steak burritos

serves 4   prep time 25 minutes   cook time 15 minutes

Wrap up the week with these easy steak and mixed pepper burritos for a tasty Tex-Mex fakeaway treat – perfect for a quick Friday night dinner.

1 tablespoon ground cumin

1 tablespoon smoked paprika

400g lean beef rump steak, fat trimmed

Calorie controlled cooking spray

2 each red and yellow peppers, deseeded and sliced

100g cooked brown rice

2 tablespoons finely chopped fresh coriander

Grated zest of 1 lime and juice of ½, plus extra lime wedges to serve

4 x 64g wholemeal tortilla wraps

½ Little Gem lettuce, shredded

1 large vine tomato, deseeded and finely chopped

4 tablespoons reduced-fat soured cream

1   Mix the cumin and paprika together, then sprinkle half of the mixture over the steak and season to taste. Mist a large frying pan with cooking spray and set over a high heat. Cook the steaks for 2½-3 minutes on each side, or to your liking, then transfer to a plate and loosely cover with foil.

2   Mist the pan again and fry the peppers for 5-6 minutes until they start to soften, then add the remaining spices and cook for another minute. Remove the pan from the heat and set aside.

3   Mix the rice with most of the coriander and the lime zest. Cut the steaks into 1cm-thick slices. Lay a wrap on the work surface and spoon a quarter of the rice down the left-hand side of the wrap, leaving a gap at the top and bottom. Top with a quarter of the lettuce, steak, peppers and tomato, followed by the soured cream.

4   Scatter over the remaining coriander and add the lime juice. Roll up the wraps and serve immediately with extra lime wedges to squeeze over.

 SmartPoints value per serving

Cook's tip

You could use sliced skinless chicken breast fillet instead of steak, instead for a total of 8 SmartPoints per serving.

Sticky barbecued chicken

serves 4   prep time 20 minutes   cook time 45 minutes

Takeaway chicken never tasted this good! These lightly spiced drumsticks go perfectly with our easy coleslaw and roasted sweet potato wedges.

600g sweet potatoes, cut into 3cm wedges

Calorie controlled cooking spray

2 teaspoons ground cumin

1 teaspoon smoked paprika

4 sachets Weight Watchers Smoky BBQ Sauce

Grated zest of ½ orange

8 chicken drumsticks, skin removed

2 spring onions, trimmed and finely sliced

1 lemon, cut into wedges to serve

FOR THE COLESLAW

80g fat-free natural yogurt

Juice of ½ lemon

½ small garlic clove, crushed

1 tablespoon finely chopped mint

100g red cabbage, finely shredded

2 carrots, peeled and grated

1 Preheat the oven to 200°C, fan 180°C, gas mark 6. Mist the sweet potato wedges with cooking spray and toss with the spices. Arrange in a single layer on a baking sheet, then bake for 45 minutes, turning halfway through, until the wedges are tender and golden.

2 Put the barbecue sauce and orange zest in a shallow baking dish. Add the chicken and turn to coat, then put in the oven and cook alongside the sweet potato wedges for the last 25 minutes of their cooking time or until the chicken is cooked through. Baste the chicken occasionally with the sauce in the baking dish.

3 Meanwhile, to make the coleslaw, combine the yogurt, lemon juice, garlic and mint in a mixing bowl and season to taste. Add the cabbage and carrots, then toss until well coated. Serve the chicken with the coleslaw and spring onions, with the lemon wedges on the side.

7 **SmartPoints value per serving**

Cook's tip

Use normal skin-on potatoes, instead of sweet potatoes, for 6 SmartPoints. per serving.

Tomato & mushroom pizza

serves 4   **prep time 15 minutes**   **cook time 20 minutes**

Fancy a pizza in a hurry? This super-simple pizza base is really quick to make – there are just two ingredients and there's no need for proving.

180g 0% fat natural Greek yogurt
180g self-raising flour
100g passata
1 garlic clove, crushed
1 tablespoon finely chopped basil, plus extra leaves to serve
80g light mozzarella, thinly sliced
100g mushrooms, sliced
2 large vine tomatoes, thinly sliced
Green salad, to serve

1   Preheat the oven to 220°C, fan 200°C, gas mark 7. Put a baking sheet in the oven to heat up. Mix the yogurt and flour together until a dough forms, then roughly shape into a ball. Roll the dough out on a piece of nonstick baking paper until roughly 30cm in diameter and bake for 10 minutes.

2   Meanwhile, mix the passata, garlic and basil together and season well. Spread over the cooked dough, leaving a 2-3cm border around the edge. Arrange the mozzarella, mushrooms and tomatoes evenly over the top.

3   Reduce the heat to 200°C, fan 180°C, gas mark 6 and bake for another 8-10 minutes. Scatter with extra basil leaves and serve with a green salad.

 SmartPoints value per serving

Cook's tip
Most veg are zero SmartPoints, so why not change up the toppings? Sliced courgettes, peppers or roasted butternut squash would all be great.

Beef ramen

serves 4   **prep time 10 minutes**   **cook time 10 minutes**

This hearty beef and noodle soup is packed with Japanese-inspired flavours.
It's perfect for when you want a meal on the table in less than half an hour.

40g dried shiitake mushrooms
500g udon noodles
**1 litre beef stock, made with
1 stock cube**
1 tablespoon tamarind paste
1 tablespoon miso paste
2 teaspoons caster sugar
**1 tablespoon sriracha, or other hot
chilli sauce**
2 teaspoons vegetable oil
**2 x 225g lean sirloin steaks,
trimmed of fat**
200g bean sprouts
**Large handful fresh coriander
leaves, roughly chopped, to garnish**
**2 spring onions, trimmed and
sliced, to garnish**
**1 tablespoon toasted sesame seeds,
to garnish**

1   Put the mushrooms in a bowl and pour over 500ml boiling water. Leave to soak for 5-6 minutes. Drain, reserving the soaking liquid, and chop any larger mushrooms. Set aside.

2   Meanwhile, cook the noodles to pack instructions and heat the stock in a large pan. Stir the tamarind and miso pastes into the stock, then add the sugar and sriracha and bring to a simmer. Add the mushrooms and the reserved liquid and warm over a gentle heat.

3   Heat the oil in a large frying pan over a high heat. Season the steaks to taste and cook for 3 minutes on each side, or to your liking. Transfer to a plate and set aside to rest for 5 minutes, then cut into 2cm-thick slices.

4   Meanwhile, add the cooked udon noodles to the stock and heat through.

5   Divide the bean sprouts between 4 large, deep bowls and ladle over the broth and noodles. Top with the sliced sirloin and serve garnished with the coriander, spring onions and a sprinkling of sesame seeds.

Cook's tip

To toast sesame seeds,
put them in a dry frying pan
over a medium heat for 3-4
minutes, stirring constantly,
until golden brown.

   SmartPoints value per serving

Sweet & sour pork with egg fried rice

serves 4   **prep time 20 minutes**   **cook time 25 minutes**

Our version of the Chinese takeaway classic has all of the sweet and sour flavours you love, but with fewer SmartPoints.

Calorie controlled cooking spray

500g pork tenderloin, fat trimmed and cut into 3cm cubes

1 red onion, finely sliced

2 red peppers and 1 green pepper, deseeded and roughly chopped

200g fresh pineapple chunks

60ml rice wine vinegar

2½ tablespoons clear honey

1 tablespoon cornflour

1 tablespoon soy sauce

1 spring onion, trimmed and sliced lengthways, to garnish

FOR THE EGG FRIED RICE

240g brown rice

Calorie controlled cooking spray

½ tablespoon soy sauce

1 spring onion, trimmed and finely chopped

100g frozen peas

2 eggs, lightly beaten

1   Cook the rice to pack instructions, then drain and set aside.

2   Meanwhile, mist a frying pan with cooking spray and cook the pork over a medium-high heat for 7-8 minutes until browned, then transfer to a plate and drain any liquid from the pan. Mist the pan again, add the onion and peppers and cook for 6-8 minutes until soft. Add the pineapple for another minute, then transfer to the plate with the pork.

3   In a small jug, mix the rice wine vinegar, honey, cornflour and soy sauce with 100ml water. Pour the sauce into the cooking pan and cook over a low heat, stirring, for 3-4 minutes. Return the pork and vegetables and pineapple to the pan and cook for another 4-5 minutes, until the sauce has thickened and the pork is cooked through.

4   Meanwhile, prepare the egg fried rice. Mist another frying pan with cooking spray, add the cooked rice and fry for 3-4 minutes, then add the soy sauce, the chopped spring onion and the peas, and stir to combine. Push the fried rice to one side of the pan and pour the eggs into the space. Leave to cook for 1 minute until just set, then scramble them and mix into the rice.

5   Serve the pork garnished with the sliced spring onion, with the egg fried rice on the side.

Cook's tip
Try this recipe using diced skinless chicken breast fillets instead of pork for 9 SmartPoints per serving.

11   **SmartPoints value per serving**

Lamb doner kebabs

serves 4   prep time 20 minutes   cook time 25 minutes + cooling

Give the kebab shop a miss and make your own! This clever take on doner kebabs served in pitta with a yogurt dressing couldn't be easier.

400g 10% fat lamb mince
2 garlic cloves, crushed
1 teaspoon cumin seeds
2 teaspoons ground coriander
½ tablespoon smoked paprika
Calorie controlled cooking spray
100g fat-free natural yogurt
Juice of ½ lemon, plus extra wedges to serve
4 x 60g pitta breads, split
½ iceberg lettuce, leaves separated
1 large vine tomato, chopped
½ red onion, finely sliced
¼ cucumber, finely sliced
50g red cabbage, shredded
Small handful each fresh parsley and fresh mint, roughly chopped

1   Preheat the oven to 200°C, fan 180°C, gas mark 6. Put the lamb mince, garlic and spices in a mixing bowl and season to taste. Mix together using your hands until well combined.

2   Mist a 900g loaf tin with cooking spray and fill with the lamb mixture, pressing it down firmly and making sure the top is level. Bake for 25 minutes, then remove from the oven and set aside to cool in the tin for 10 minutes.

3   Combine the yogurt and lemon juice in a small bowl. Stuff each pitta with a quarter of the lettuce, tomatoes, onion, cucumber and cabbage.

4   Turn the lamb out onto a chopping board and slice thinly. Add a quarter of the lamb to each pitta, then top with the yogurt dressing and some fresh parsley and mint, and serve with the lemon wedges.

9   **SmartPoints value per serving**

Cook's tip

Use Weight Watchers Wraps instead of pitta if you prefer, for a total of 8 SmartPoints per serving.

Thai prawn curry with noodles

serves 4   prep time 5 minutes   cook time 15 minutes

A fakeaway favourite with all the fragrant and fiery flavours of a Thai green curry. Serve it with noodles, for a change from the usual rice.

100g Thai green curry paste

200ml reduced-fat coconut milk

450ml vegetable stock, made with 1 stock cube

150g green beans, trimmed and halved

150g Tenderstem broccoli, halved

150g sugar snap peas, halved

2 small pak choi, halved

300g raw king prawns

Juice of ½ lime, plus extra wedges to serve

150g rice noodles

1 red chilli, finely sliced

Small handful fresh coriander

1   Put the curry paste in a large pan and cook over a medium heat for 2 minutes, stirring occasionally, then add the coconut milk and stock and gently simmer for 5 minutes.

2   Add the beans and cook for 2 minutes, then add the broccoli, and cook for 4 minutes. Turn the heat off and stir in the sugar snaps, pak choi and prawns. Allow the prawns to cook in the residual heat for 2 minutes, then stir in the lime juice.

3   Meanwhile, cook the noodles according to pack instructions, then drain and toss with a squeeze of lime. Serve the curry with the noodles in the same bowl and top generously with chilli, coriander leaves and extra lime wedges to squeeze over.

 SmartPoints value per serving

Quesadillas

These Mexican toasted wraps make great family dinners. Change up the fillings to keep the idea fresh with these brilliant yet simple variations.

Roast vegetable quesadillas

serves 4   prep time 10 minutes
cook time 55 minutes

Preheat the oven to 220°C, fan 200°C, gas mark 7. Spread 1 diced **aubergine**, 1 diced **courgette**, 1 deseeded and diced **yellow pepper** and 1 diced **red onion** on a baking sheet and mist with **calorie controlled cooking spray**. Scatter over 1 teaspoon **dried mixed herbs** and toss to combine, then season to taste. Roast for 15 minutes, then add 110g halved **cherry tomatoes** and roast for a further 10 minutes until the veg is tender. Grate 100g **half-fat Cheddar cheese** and scatter half of it over 2 x **Weight Watchers Wraps**. Top with the roasted veg, then scatter over the remaining cheese. Top each quesadilla with a second tortilla, pressing down gently. Mist a frying pan with cooking spray and put over a medium-high heat. Cook the quesadillas one at a time for 3-4 minutes. Mist the top with more cooking spray, then flip over and cook for 3-4 minutes on the other side until golden. Quarter and serve.

 4   SmartPoints value per serving

Feta & black bean quesadillas

serves 4   prep time 10 minutes
cook time 16 minutes

Drain and rinse a 400g tin of **black beans**, then put them in a large bowl with 1 thinly sliced **red onion**, ½ teaspoon **ground cumin**, a handful of roughly chopped **fresh coriander** and the juice of **1 lime**. Crumble in 150g **light feta cheese**, then gently mix to combine everything and season to taste. Lay 2 x 64g wholemeal **tortilla wraps** on the work surface and spoon half the filling over each one. Top with 2 more wraps, then press gently together. Mist a frying pan with **calorie controlled cooking spray** and put over a medium-high heat. Add the quesadillas one at a time and cook for 3-4 minutes. Mist the top with more cooking spray, then flip over and cook for 3-4 minutes on the other until golden. Quarter and serve.

 5   SmartPoints value per serving

Pesto chicken quesadillas

serves 4   prep time 10 minutes
cook time 16 minutes

Spread 4 x 64g wholemeal **tortilla wraps** with ½ tablespoon **reduced-fat green pesto** each. Shred 150g **cooked skinless chicken breast** and divide between 2 of the wraps, then scatter 125g sliced **light mozzarella**, 8 quartered **cherry tomatoes** and a small handful of **fresh basil leaves** on top of the chicken. Top with the 2 remaining tortillas, pesto-side down, pressing down lightly. Mist a large frying pan with **calorie controlled cooking spray** and put over a medium-high heat. Add the quesadillas one at a time and cook for 3-4 minutes. Mist the top with more cooking spray, then flip over and cook for 3-4 minutes on the other until golden. Quarter and serve.

 5   SmartPoints value per serving

Steak & pepper quesadillas

serves 4   prep time 10 minutes
cook time 30 minutes

Mist a frying pan with **calorie controlled cooking spray** and put over a medium-high heat. Add 175g lean, **thin-cut steak** and cook for 2 minutes on each side, or until done to your liking. Transfer to a plate to rest for 10 minutes. Mist the pan again with cooking spray. Deseed and slice 1 **red pepper** and 1 **yellow pepper** and add it to the pan, along with 1 sliced **red onion**. Cook for 6-8 minutes or until tender. Add 1 finely chopped **garlic clove** and ½ teaspoon **dried chilli flakes** and cook for 1 minute. Cut the steak into strips and mix it with the peppers and onion. Grate 100g **half-fat Cheddar cheese** and scatter half of it over 2 x **Weight Watchers Wraps**. Top with the steak and veg, then sprinkle over the remaining cheese and a small handful of fresh coriander leaves. Top with 2 more wraps, pressing down gently. Mist the pan with cooking spray and put over a medium-high heat. Cook the quesadillas one at a time for 3-4 minutes. Mist the top with more cooking spray, then flip over and cook for 3-4 minutes on the other side until golden. Quarter and serve.

5   SmartPoints value per serving

Desserts & bakes

Apple & rhubarb crumble

serves 6   prep time 20 minutes   cook time 50 minutes

Juicy apples, tangy rhubarb and a crispy oat topping make the perfect combination in this ever-popular pud. Serve it warm with custard for an extra treat.

3 apples, peeled, cored and sliced

400g rhubarb, trimmed and cut into 2cm pieces

2 tablespoons caster sugar

Grated zest and juice of 1 orange

400g tin low-fat custard

FOR THE CRUMBLE TOPPING

75g plain flour

50g low-fat spread, cut into small cubes

25g light brown soft sugar

75g porridge oats

1   Preheat the oven to 180°C, fan 160°C, gas mark 4. Put the fruit, caster sugar and orange zest into a large ovenproof dish and toss together. Add the orange juice, then cover the dish with foil and cook for 25 minutes, or until the fruit is soft.

2   Meanwhile, in a mixing bowl, rub the flour and low-fat spread together until the mixture resembles coarse breadcrumbs. Stir in the sugar and oats, then scatter the topping over the fruit.

3   Bake for 25 minutes, or until golden. Heat the custard to pack instructions and serve with the warm crumble.

8   **SmartPoints value per serving**

Cook's tip

Instead of the custard, you could serve the crumble with 0% fat natural Greek yogurt for 6 SmartPoints per serving.

Rice pudding with honey & walnuts

serves 4   **prep time 5 minutes**   **cook time 30 minutes**

This simple, traditional dessert is easy to make and so satisfying to eat. The honey and nuts add a touch of sweetness and crunch.

10g low-fat spread
1 tablespoon caster sugar
100g pudding rice
550ml skimmed milk
Grated zest of 1 lemon
1 dried bay leaf
1 vanilla pod, split lengthways
10g walnuts
150g 0% fat natural Greek yogurt
4 teaspoons clear honey, to serve

1   Melt the spread in a large, heavy-based pan over a low-medium heat. Add the sugar and cook for 1-2 minutes, stirring, until the sugar has dissolved, then add the rice. Stir to coat, then add the milk, half the lemon zest, the bay leaf and vanilla pod.

2   Bring to the boil, then reduce the heat and simmer for about 25 minutes, stirring often, until the rice is tender and all the milk is absorbed.

3   Meanwhile, put the walnuts in a dry frying pan and cook over a medium-high heat, stirring, until just browned and fragrant, then remove from the heat and roughly chop.

4   Stir the yogurt into the rice pudding. Divide between 4 bowls and serve each with 1 teaspoon of honey, a scattering of the chopped walnuts and the remaining lemon zest.

7   **SmartPoints value per serving**

Blueberry muffins

makes 8   prep time 20 minutes   cook time 20 minutes

Perfect at breakfast time, popped into a lunchbox or enjoyed as an afternoon snack, these moist, fruity muffins are super simple to make.

150g plain flour
1 tablespoon baking powder
Pinch of salt
1 large egg
100ml skimmed milk
50g low-fat spread, melted and cooled
30g golden caster sugar
1 teaspoon vanilla extract
200g blueberries
1 tablespoon Demerara sugar

1 Preheat the oven to 200°C, fan 180°C, gas mark 6. Line a 12-hole muffin tin with 8 muffin cases.

2 Sift the flour, baking powder and salt into a large mixing bowl. In a separate large bowl, whisk together the egg, milk, melted spread, sugar and vanilla.

3 Add the dry ingredients to the wet ingredients and whisk together, but don't overmix. Fold in the blueberries.

4 Divide the mixture between the muffin cases and sprinkle with the Demerara sugar.

5 Bake for 25-30 minutes until well risen and golden, then transfer the muffins to a wire rack to cool.

The muffins will keep in an airtight container for 3-4 days.

Cook's tip
Fancy a change? You could swap the blueberries for raspberries for the same SmartPoints.

 SmartPoints value per muffin

Chocolate self-saucing pudding

serves 8   prep time 10 minutes   cook time 30 minutes

This deliciously rich, moist chocolate sponge creates its own sauce in the baking dish. Serve it warm for the perfect weekend treat.

Calorie controlled cooking spray

150g plain flour

100g caster sugar

2 teaspoons baking powder

50g cocoa powder, plus an extra 2 tablespoons for the sauce and ½ teaspoon, to serve

Pinch of salt

1 egg

150ml skimmed milk

30g low-fat spread, melted and cooled

½ teaspoon vanilla extract

30g light brown soft sugar

1   Preheat the oven to 180°C, fan 160°C, gas mark 4. Mist a 20cm baking dish with cooking spray. Sift the flour, caster sugar, baking powder, 50g cocoa powder and the salt into a large mixing bowl.

2   In a separate bowl, lightly beat the egg, then whisk in the milk, melted spread and vanilla extract. Fold the wet ingredients into the dry ingredients until combined. Pour the mixture into the baking dish.

3   In a small jug, combine the brown sugar with 2 tablespoons cocoa powder and sprinkle over the top of the pudding mixture. Carefully pour over 300ml boiling water, then bake for 25-30 minutes until the top of the pudding feels firm and springy. Dust with the extra ½ teaspoon cocoa powder, then serve.

8   **SmartPoints value per serving**

Cook's tip

Make this extra-special by serving it with fresh berries and a dollop of 0% fat natural Greek yogurt for no extra SmartPoints.

Apple tarte tatin

serves 6   prep time 20 minutes   cook time 35 minutes

Ready-made pastry makes this French-inspired tart simplicity itself. The tangy crème fraîche is the perfect accompaniment to the caramelised apples.

3 Braeburn apples, peeled, cored and cut into 8 wedges each
30g low-fat spread
25g light brown soft sugar
Calorie controlled cooking spray
175g ready-rolled light puff pastry
150g half-fat crème fraîche

1   Preheat the oven to 200°C, fan 180°C, gas mark 6. Put the apples and 1 tablespoon water in a large lidded frying pan and set over a low heat. Cover and simmer for 10 minutes, swirling the pan occasionally, until the apples are tender.

2   Drain any excess liquid from the pan, then add the low-fat spread and brown sugar. Swirl the pan and increase the heat, simmering for 5 minutes until the apples are coated in the caramelised sugar. Mist a 20cm circular pie dish with cooking spray and arrange the apples over the base.

3   Cut the pastry into a circle large enough to cover the top of the pie dish, discarding the trimmings. Place the pastry circle over the apples, tucking the edges inside the dish. Make a small cut in the top to release any steam when baking.

4   Put the tin on a baking sheet and bake for 20 minutes or until the pastry is puffed and deeply golden. Leave to stand for 5 minutes, then invert the tart onto a heatproof serving plate and serve with the crème fraîche.

 SmartPoints value per serving

Spiced ginger scones

makes 10   prep time 15 minutes   cook time 15 minutes

Nothing beats a warm scone, fresh from the oven, for an afternoon teatime treat.
These are flavoured with stem ginger to make them even more special.

Calorie controlled cooking spray
115g wholemeal plain flour
**115g white plain flour, plus extra
for dusting**
1½ teaspoons baking powder
1 teaspoon mixed spice
75g low-fat spread
40g caster sugar
40g stem ginger, finely diced
2 large eggs
3 tablespoons buttermilk

1   Preheat the oven to 190°C, fan 170°C, gas mark 5. Mist a nonstick baking
    sheet with cooking spray.

2   Sift the flours, baking powder and mixed spice into a large mixing
    bowl. Using your fingertips, rub in the low-fat spread until the mixture
    resembles coarse breadcrumbs.

3   Stir in the sugar and stem ginger. Lightly beat 1 of the eggs and add
    to the dry ingredients with the buttermilk, mixing quickly with a table
    knife. Form into a soft dough using your hands.

4   Lightly flour the work surface and gently roll out the dough until it's
    1½cm thick. Cut out 10 rounds using a 6cm cutter dipped in flour.
    Transfer the scones to the baking sheet.

5   Lightly beat the remaining egg in a small bowl and use a pastry brush to
    brush the top of each scone with the beaten egg. Bake for 10-15 minutes
    until risen and golden, then transfer to a wire rack to cool slightly
    before serving.

 5 SmartPoints value per scone

Cook's tip
Serve each scone with
1 teaspoon low-calorie jam
and 1 tablespoon half-fat
crème fraîche for an extra
3 SmartPoints per serving.

Sticky pudding

serves 12   prep time 15 minutes + cooling   cook time 30 minutes

A delicious, moist pud flavoured with ginger and topped with apple crisps. This traybake-style dessert serves 12, so it's perfect for a big family dinner.

3 small red apples, 2 peeled and grated (about 170g), one left whole

Calorie controlled cooking spray

180g soft prunes, roughly chopped

2 teaspoons vanilla extract

3 teaspoons freshly grated ginger

6 large eggs, separated

250g self-raising flour

2 teaspoons bicarbonate of soda

Pinch of salt

280g date syrup

1   Preheat the oven to 140°C, fan 120°C, gas mark 1 and line a baking sheet with baking paper. Halve and thinly slice the whole apple, then spread the slices out on the baking sheet and bake for 40 minutes or until crisp.

2   Increase the oven temperature to 180°C, fan 160°C, gas mark 4. Mist a 30cm x 20cm cake tin with cooking spray and line the base and sides with baking paper.

3   Put the prunes and the 2 grated apples in a pan with 450ml water and bring to a simmer, then cover and cook for 5-6 minutes until softened. Set aside for 5 minutes to cool slightly, then transfer to a blender, add the vanilla extract and ginger, and blitz to a smooth purée.

4   Transfer the prune mixture to a mixing bowl and stir in the egg yolks. Sift in the flour, add the bicarbonate of soda and the salt, then stir well to combine.

5   Whisk the egg whites in a clean bowl until stiff peaks form, then gently fold into the pudding mixture, ensuring they are fully incorporated. Pour the mixture into the prepared tin and bake for 25-30 minutes, or until a skewer inserted into the centre of the pudding comes out clean.

6   Reserve 2 tablespoons of the date syrup, then put the rest in a small pan and warm over a low heat until runny. Poke holes all over the pudding with a skewer, then drizzle the warmed syrup all over the top while still warm. Remove from the tin and cut into 12 squares. Serve topped with the apple crisps and drizzled with the reserved date syrup.

Any leftover pudding will keep in the fridge for 2 days.

Cook's tip

You could serve this with 100g low-fat custard per person for a total of 11 SmartPoints per serving.

7   **SmartPoints value per serving**

Steamed lemon pudding

serves 8   prep time 15 minutes   cook time 1 hour 30 minutes

Want the perfect dessert for a chilly evening? Try this warming, wintry steamed pud that's flavoured with lemon curd and served with homemade custard.

Calorie controlled cooking spray
3 tablespoons lemon curd
Pared zest of 1 lemon
80g low-fat spread
30g caster sugar
2 eggs
120g self-raising flour
1 teaspoon baking powder
75g fat-free natural yogurt

FOR THE CUSTARD
1 egg yolk
10g caster sugar
2 teaspoons custard powder
170ml skimmed milk

1   Mist a 1-litre pudding basin with cooking spray, line the bottom with a circle of baking paper and spoon in the lemon curd and half the lemon zest.

2   Put the spread, sugar, eggs, flour, baking powder, yogurt and the remaining lemon zest in a mixing bowl and whisk together until just combined, then spoon the mixture over the lemon curd. Cover the top of the basin with a layer of baking paper and a layer of kitchen foil, then tie it tightly around the rim of the basin with kitchen string.

3   Put the basin in a large pan on a trivet. Fill the pan with boiling water until it comes halfway up the pudding basin, then put the lid on and cook over a low heat for 1 hour 30 minutes, topping up the water if you need to.

4   While the pudding is cooking, make the custard. Mix the egg yolk, caster sugar and custard powder in a small bowl to a smooth paste. Warm the milk in a pan over a low heat until just steaming, then pour a little into the egg mixture and whisk together. Pour this mixture back into the pan of milk and cook over a low heat for 15 minutes, stirring often until thick enough to coat the back of a spoon.

5   Remove the foil and baking paper from the pudding. The sponge should spring back when gently pressed with your finger. Using oven gloves, put a plate on top of the basin and carefully invert to turn out the pudding onto the plate. Spoon any remaining lemon curd over the pudding and serve with the custard.

6 SmartPoints value per serving

Earl Grey fruit loaf

serves 12   prep time 20 minutes + soaking   cook time 1 hour 10 minutes

A delicious traditional-style fruity loaf cake flavoured with Earl Grey tea and cinnamon. Slice it up for a family picnic or serve it when friends visit for afternoon tea.

125g raisins

125g sultanas

50g chopped candied peel

50g glacé cherries,
roughly chopped

30g Demerara sugar

150ml hot Earl Grey tea, made
with 2 tea bags

Calorie controlled cooking spray

2 large eggs

225g self-raising flour

1 teaspoon ground cinnamon

Grated zest of 1 orange

1   Put the raisins, sultanas, candied peel and glacé cherries in a large mixing bowl. Reserve 1 teaspoon of the sugar, then stir the rest into the tea until dissolved and pour over the fruit. Stir to combine, cover with a cloth and leave to soak for 2-3 hours, or preferably overnight in the fridge.

2   Preheat the oven to 170°C, fan 150°C, gas mark 3. Mist a 900g nonstick loaf tin with cooking spray and line the base and sides with baking paper. In a small bowl, whisk the eggs and add to the soaked fruit. Sift in the flour and cinnamon, add the orange zest and 50ml water and stir to combine.

3   Pour the mixture into the lined loaf tin and smooth the surface, then sprinkle over the reserved Demerara sugar. Bake in the centre of the oven for 1 hour 10 minutes or until the top of the cake feels springy and a skewer inserted into the centre of the cake comes out clean.

4   Remove from the oven and turn out onto a wire rack. Leave to cool, then cut into 12 slices.

The cake can be stored in an airtight container at room temperature for 2-3 days.

Cook's tip

Try toasting a slice of the loaf and serving with 1 teaspoon of low-fat spread for an extra 1 SmartPoint per slice.

7   SmartPoints value per serving

Chocolate brownies

makes 16   prep time 10 minutes + cooling   cook time 20 minutes

Who doesn't love a chocolate brownie? These are made with Greek yogurt, which keeps them nice and moist, while chocolate chips make them even more indulgent.

Calorie controlled cooking spray
90g cocoa powder
150g caster sugar
½ teaspoon baking powder
¼ teaspoon salt
200g 0% fat natural Greek yogurt
2 large eggs, lightly beaten
2 teaspoons vanilla extract
25g dark chocolate chips

1   Preheat the oven to 190°C, fan 170°C, gas mark 5. Mist a 20cm square cake tin with cooking spray and line the bottom with baking paper.

2   Put the cocoa powder, sugar, baking powder and salt in a mixing bowl and stir to combine, then stir in the yogurt, eggs and vanilla extract until well combined.

3   Stir in the chocolate chips, then spoon the mixture into the prepared tin and level the top with the back of the spoon. Bake for 20 minutes, then allow to cool in the tin for 15 minutes before turning out and cutting into 16 squares.

The brownies will keep in an airtight container for 2 days.

3   SmartPoints value per brownie

Cook's tip
If you're not a fan of dark chocolate, you can use milk or white chocolate chips for the same SmartPoints.

Fruit trifle

serves 8   prep time 5 minutes + chilling   cook time 25 minutes

Trifle is a great special occasion dessert and is really simple to put together. Succulent summer fruits, jelly and sponge cake are topped with vanilla custard and Greek yogurt.

4 sheets gelatine
500g frozen summer fruits
3 tablespoons clear honey
5 trifle sponges
1 egg yolk
20g caster sugar
2 teaspoons custard powder
350ml skimmed milk
1 teaspoon vanilla bean paste or vanilla extract
150g half-fat crème fraîche
400g 0% fat natural Greek yogurt

1   Put three sheets of the gelatine in a small bowl of cold water. Reserve 2 tablespoons of the fruit for decoration, then put the rest into a pan with the honey and a splash of water and cook over a low heat for 10 minutes until the fruit is breaking apart. Set aside to cool for 10 minutes.

2   Remove the gelatine from the bowl and squeeze to drain off any excess water, then stir into the fruit mixture until dissolved.

3   Arrange the trifle sponges over the bottom of a small trifle dish. Pour the fruit and gelatine mixture over the sponges and put in the fridge for 1 hour to set.

4   Meanwhile, put the remaining gelatine sheet in a small bowl of cold water. Put the egg yolk, caster sugar and custard powder in another small bowl and mix to a smooth paste.

5   Put the milk and vanilla bean paste or extract in a pan and set over a low-medium heat until just steaming, then pour a little of the warmed milk into the egg yolk mixture and whisk together. Pour the egg mixture back into the pan of milk and cook over a low heat for 15 minutes, stirring often, until it's thick enough to coat the back of a spoon.

6   Set the custard aside for 10 minutes to cool slightly. Squeeze out any excess water from the last sheet of the gelatine and add to the custard, stirring until dissolved, then whisk in the crème fraîche. Pour the custard over the jelly and return to the fridge for 1 hour, or until set.

7   Top the set custard with the yogurt, decorate with the reserved fruit and serve immediately.

(7)   SmartPoints value per serving

Cookies

Fancy a bit of baking? Whip up a batch of basic cookie dough, then use it to make these four delicious varieties – which one will you choose to go with your afternoon cuppa?

To make the cookie dough

Using a stand mixer, cream 100g **low-fat spread**, 125g **golden caster sugar** and 75g **light brown soft sugar** in a large mixing bowl until smooth and thick. Beat in 1 **egg** and ½ teaspoon **vanilla extract**, then sift in 200g **self-raising flour** and a large pinch of **salt** and mix until just combined.

Chocolate chip

makes 16   prep time 10 minutes + chilling   cook time 12 minutes

Make the basic cookie dough as above, then stir 70g **milk chocolate chips** into the mixture. Cover and chill for 3 hours. Preheat the oven to 200°C, fan 180°C, gas mark 6. Line two baking sheets with baking paper. Form the mixture into 16 walnut-sized balls and put them on the sheets, leaving plenty of room for the cookies to spread. Use the back of a wet spoon to flatten the tops of the cookies slightly, then bake for 10-12 minutes or until golden at the edges. Leave the cookies on the baking tray for 5 minutes to firm up, then transfer to a wire rack to cool completely.

 6   SmartPoints value per cookie

Peanut butter

makes 16   prep time 10 minutes + chilling   cook time 12 minutes

Make the basic cookie dough as above, then add 65g crunchy **peanut butter** and mix until combined. Cover and chill for 3 hours. Preheat the oven to 200°C, fan 180°C, gas mark 6. Line two baking sheets with baking paper. Form the mixture into 16 walnut-sized balls and put them on the sheets, leaving plenty of room for the cookies to spread. Use the back of a wet spoon to flatten the tops of the cookies slightly, then bake for 10-12 minutes or until golden at the edges. Leave the cookies on the baking tray for 5 minutes to firm up, then transfer to a wire rack to cool completely.

 6   SmartPoints value per cookie

Spiced orange & cranberry

makes 16   prep time 10 minutes + chilling   cook time 12 minutes

Make the basic cookie dough as above, then add 75g **dried cranberries**, ½ teaspoon **ground ginger** and the grated zest of 1 **orange** to the mixture and mix until combined. Cover and chill for 3 hours. Preheat the oven to 200°C, fan 180°C, gas mark 6. Line two baking sheets with baking paper. Form the mixture into 16 walnut-sized balls and put them on the sheets, leaving plenty of room for the cookies to spread. Use the back of a wet spoon to flatten the tops of the cookies slightly, then bake for 10-12 minutes or until golden at the edges. Leave the cookies on the baking tray for 5 minutes to firm up, then transfer to a wire rack to cool completely.

 6   SmartPoints value per cookie

Oat & raisin

makes 16   prep time 10 minutes + chilling   cook time 12 minutes

Make the basic cookie dough as above, then add 50g **porridge oats** and 75g **raisins** to the mixture and mix until combined. Cover and chill for 3 hours. Preheat the oven to 200°C, fan 180°C, gas mark 6. Line 2 baking sheets with baking paper. Form the mixture into 16 walnut-sized balls and put them on the sheets, leaving plenty of room for the cookies to spread. Use the back of a wet spoon to flatten the tops of the cookies slightly, then bake for 10-12 minutes or until golden at the edges. Leave the cookies on the baking tray for 5 minutes to firm up, then transfer to a wire rack to cool completely.

 6   SmartPoints value per cookie

Recipe index